When a Bully is President
Truth and Creativity for Oppressive Times

Cuando El Presidente es un Bulí
La Verdad y la Creatividad en Tiempos Opresivos

by/por Maya Gonzalez

Voice is a Revolution

How this Book came to be....

This book was conceived on November 9, 2016 with the publishing date of February 20, 2017. That means it took under 4 months to write, illustrate, translate, design and publish the book you're holding in your hands right now. As radical indie-publishers we want to be responsive to our communities and push the limits of what's possible in publishing.

How did we do it? To begin, we used a template I had already designed for our *Make Books Now Indie Publisher Training* program. Next, I used the easiest, most accessible art materials and style possible. All of the art is made on 8 ½" x 11", white cardstock paper using a fountain pen, archival markers and watercolors. The style is super easy and fast to create. We believe our kids can't wait for books about the things affecting their lives right now. Owning our own press is an important step towards mobility, #ownvoices and true creative power rising.

We are in serious need of more books by and about People of Color and Indigenous People. We've created an online school and a free online kids program to begin learning more about how to create your own books.

Honing our skills alongside our hearts and spirits helps us produce strong, deep children's books quickly and effectively for our communities and support the flow of truth, respect and love that we need in these days. It's never too early or too late to begin. You are the storyteller. You are the artist. Join the revolution now!
www.reflectionpress.com/radicalact

Story & Art Copyright © 2017 by Maya Christina Gonzalez
Translated by Marta Huante Robles
Published by Reflection Press, San Francisco, CA

Reflection Press is an independent publisher of radical and revolutionary children's books and works that expand cultural and spiritual awareness. **www.reflectionpress.com**

ISBN 978-1-945289-02-6 (paperback)
Library of Congress Control Number: 2017930477
Book Design by Matthew SG
Special thanks to Dana Goldberg for reviewing the Spanish
and to our Indiegogo supporters
who helped make this book happen.

When a Bully is President
Cuando El Presidente es un Bulí

by/por Maya Gonzalez

translation/traducción Marta Huante Robles

We are stronger together.

We see the truth in each other.

We focus on self love and community love first.

We use our creativity to create a new reality.

Together truth, love and creativity are rising within us.

Together we are strong.

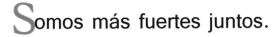

Somos más fuertes juntos.

Vemos la verdad uno en sí.

Enfocamos en amor propio y amor comunitario antes de todo.

Usamos nuestra creatividad para crear una nueva realidad.

Juntos la verdad, el amor y la creatividad están creciendo dentro de nosotros.

Juntos somos fuertes.

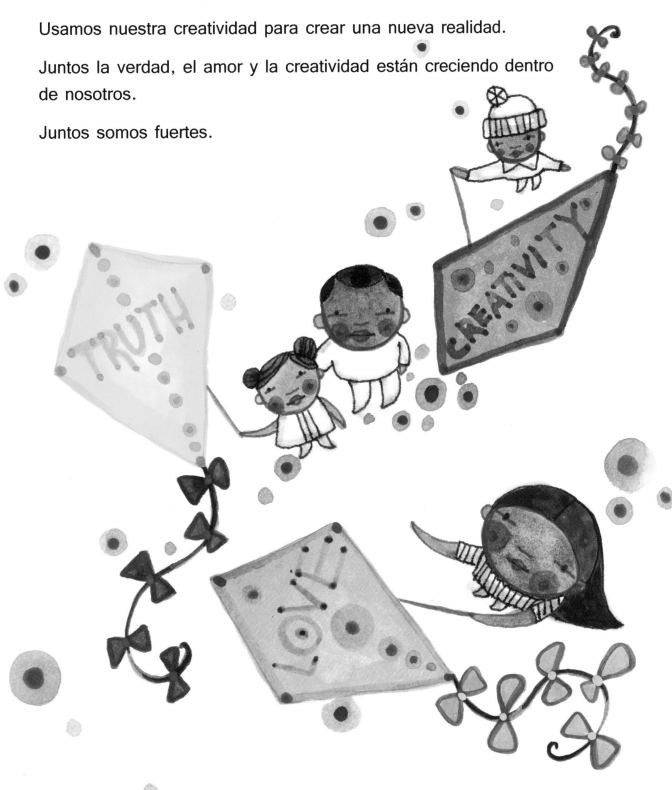

Juntos miramos y vemos ¿QUÉ ES UN BULÍ?
Ver nos mantiene fuertes.

Un bulí es alguien que usa su fuerza o su control para asustar a alguien, especialmente a obligar una persona a comportar de la manera que el bulí quiere. Esto puede extenderse de la palabra hablada a la acción física al silencio. El propósito del bulí-ing es lastimar el corazón y el espíritu incluso sin dañar el cuerpo.

Together we look and see WHAT A BULLY IS.
Seeing keeps us strong.

A bully is someone who uses their strength or control to frighten someone, especially to force a person to act the way the bully wants. This can range from spoken word to physical action to silence. The purpose of bullying is to hurt the heart and spirit even if the body is not hurt.

Juntos miramos y vemos **LA HISTORIA y LOS COMPORTAMIENTOS DEL BULÍ.** Ver nos mantiene fuertes.

Tristemente, la historia de nuestro propio país, los Estados Unidos, está basada en una fuerte forma de bulí-ing llamada la colonización.

Llegó gente de Europa a este continente y la quería por su cuenta. Ellos acosaron a los indígenas americanos quienes siempre habían vivido aquí de sus tierras. Muchos americanos nativos perdieron sus vidas o fueron matados a través de campañas para expulsarlos de su casa y destruir su forma de vivir.

Together we look and see
BULLY HISTORY and BEHAVIORS.
Seeing keeps us strong.

Sadly, our own US history is rooted in a strong form of bullying called colonization.

People came from Europe to this continent and wanted it for their own. They bullied the American Indians who had always lived here off their land. Many Native American people lost their lives or were killed through campaigns to drive them out of their home and destroy their way of living.

Washington/317 people   Jefferson/200 people   Madison/100+ people   Monroe/75 people

Jackson/200 people   Van Buren/1 person   Harrison/11 people   Tyler/70 people   Polk/25 people

Taylor/150+ people   Johnson/8 people   Grant/5 people

Las gentes que vinieron a este continente querían gran riqueza y control.

Ellos intimidaron a los africanos a que les trabajaran en esclavitud. 12 de los primeros 18 presidentes fueron dueños y tomaron como su propiedad a gente africana. Muchos afroamericanos perdieron sus vidas o fueron matados a causa de la institución americana de la esclavitud.

The people who came to this continent wanted great wealth and control.

They bullied Africans to work for them as slaves. 12 of the first 18 presidents owned African people as property. Many African Americans lost their lives or were killed through the American institution of slavery.

Y de Texas a California, México fue empujado a la guerra para que los EEUU podrían apoderarse de más tierras.

Después, mexicanos ya viviendo sobre esta tierra se convirtieron en ciudadanos de segunda clase de los EEUU sin igualdad de derechos. Muchos mexicoamericanos fueron matados por no mantenerse en línea. Cada una de estas tres comunidades fueron acosaron para construir los que se convirtió en la tierra y base de la riqueza de los Estados Unidos.

And from Texas to California, Mexico was pushed into war so the US could get more land.

Afterwards, Mexicans already living on this land became second class citizens of the US without equal rights. Many Mexican Americans were killed if they didn't stay in line. All three of these communities were bullied to build what became America's land and wealth base.

12

La colonización es una forma muy fuerte del bulí-ing. Tan fuerte de hecho, que hoy en día seguimos viviendo en su eco.

Las tres comunidades, indígenas americanos, afroamericanos y mexicoamericanos siguen siendo acosados en los EEUU por razones de nuestra historia.

Otras comunidades que también sufren del bulí-ing en los Estados Unido son estadounidenses musulmanes y sij, estadounidenses asiáticos, y muchos emigrantes.

Y de todas las comunidades estadounidenses LGBTQ, estadounidenses discapacitados y estadounidenses que identifiquen como mujeres o niñas sufren del bulí-ing.

Colonization is a strong form of bullying. So strong in fact, that we still live in its echo.

All three of these communities, American Indians, African Americans and Mexican Americans remain bullied in the US because of our history.

Other communities bullied in the US are Muslim and Sikh Americans, Asian Americans, and many immigrants.

And from all communities LGBTQ Americans, disabled Americans and Americans who identify as women or girls are bullied.

THIS BUS IS HEADING HOME

a seat for everyone

ROSA PARKS AND
CLAUDETTE COLVIN
BUS LINE

NATIVE AMERICANS
AFRICAN AMERICANS
MEXICAN AMERICANS
CHICANX
LGBTQI2S AMERICANS
DISABLED AMERICANS
WOMEN+GIRL AMERICANS
MUSLIM+SIKH AMERICANS
AMERICANS
IMMIGRANTS
AMERICANS
BULLY
RACISM
SEXISM
TRANS PHOBIA
BULLY
ISLAMO PHOBIA
HOMO PHOBIA
BULLY
HOMO PHOBIA
BULLY
ABLEISM
MISOGINY
BULLY
RACISM
SEXISM
BULLY

¿Porque nos hace fuerte ver el bulí-ing?

Porque cuando podemos ver el cuadro grande, empezamos a ver el marco chico y el marco más pequeño hasta que finalmente podemos ver la verdad que siempre estaba allí de pie todo el rato. Juntos podemos ver que el bulí-ing no se basa en la verdad. Todo el mundo merece ser ellos mismos, en igualdad y libertad. Esa es la verdad. Cuando miramos más de cerca y más allá del bulí-ing, te vemos a TÍ. Tú eres la verdad.

Saber que tú eres la verdad te mantiene fuerte.

Why does seeing bullying keep us strong?

Because when we can see the big picture, we can begin to see the small picture and the smaller picture until finally we can see the truth that was standing there all along. Together we can see that bullying is not based in truth. Everyone deserves to be themselves, equally and freely. That is the truth. When we look closer and see through bullying, we see YOU. You are the truth.

Knowing that you are truth keeps you strong.

18

WE R THE PEOPLE

Hacer nos mantiene fuertes.

Si quieres hacer algo cuando un bulí es presidente, estas son unas cosas que los jóvenes y los niños hacen con sus familias. Aquí hay algunas cosas que puedes hacer por tu cuenta o con otros niños.

Doing keeps us strong.

If you want to do something when a bully is president, here are some things young people and kids do with their families. Here are some things you can do on your own or with other kids.

EQUITY

HOMES for everyone

water is LIFE

IMMIGRANTS' RIGHTS

ENVIRONMENTAL PROTECTION

INDIGENOUS Rights

everything is connected

Ser nos fortalece.

Aunque no hagas nada acerca de un bulí siendo presidente, sigues haciendo algo. Tú sigues siendo tú. Tú sigues siendo tu verdad. Necesitamos tú verdad. Recuerda siempre que eres importante. Esto nos fortalece a todos.

Being keeps us strong.

Even if you don't do anything about a bully being president, you're still doing something. You are being you. You are being your truth. We need the truth of you. Always remember that you are important. This keeps all of us strong.

Conociendo cómo funcionan las cosas también te fortalece.

Cuando un bulí es presidente, los que son como esa persona puedan sentirse que tienen más razón para acosar a los demás. Puede que veas más bulí-ing.

Es importante que nadie se lastime, pero no existe razón para convencer a un bulí de cualquier cosa mientras están bulí-ing. Es como si no te pudieran oír. Es mejor dejarlos a solas con su bulí-ing y cuidar de ti mismo y de tus amigos o familiares. ¡Aléjate y haz tu propia honda! Deja que el bulí haga lo suyo. Esto te mantiene fuerte.

Knowing the way things work keeps you strong too.

When a bully is president, people who are like that person may feel like they have more reason to bully. You may see more bullying.

It's important that no one gets hurt, but there's no reason to convince a bully of anything while they're bullying. It's like they can't hear you. It's best to leave them alone with their bullying and take care of yourself and your friends or family. Walk away and do your own thing! Leave the bully to their own thing. This keeps you strong.

Ser acosado por un bulí se siente horrible. Puede sentirse pesado, hasta cansa, en especial cuando es parte de una larga historia de bulí-ing. No tienes que desquitarte de estos sentimientos. Hace perfecto sentido sentirlos. Puede que eres parte de un gran legado de sentimientos. Puedes llamarles a tus antepasados cuando te dejes sentir estos sentimientos dentro de ti. Busca donde puedes sentirlos. Siente te. Y deja que tus sentimientos y tus antepasados te mantengan fuerte.

● ◆ ●

Being bullied feels crummy. It can feel heavy, even tiring, especially when it's part of a long history of bullying. You don't need to push these feelings away. It makes perfect sense to feel them. You may be part of a long lineage of feelings. You will call in your ancestors when you let these feelings be within you. Find a place where you can feel them. Feel you. And let your feelings and your ancestors keep you strong.

feelings

Puede parecer mucho. Lo más que puedas ver el bulí-ing lo más que puedas ver los diferentes tamaños en que se presenta, desde lo más grande como la colonización, hasta el bulí-ing que ocurre en el pasillo en la escuela o en tu vecindario. Y TODO necesita cambiar.

¿De verdad puede un niño hacer una diferencia?

La respuesta es sí.

It can seem like a lot. The more you see bullying the more you can see the different sizes it comes in, from very large like colonization, all the way down to bullying in the hallway at school or even in your neighborhood. And it ALL needs to change.

Can a kid really make a difference?

The answer is yes.

Tomará tiempo.
Pero juntos somos fuertes y eso te incluye a ti.

Gloria Anzaldúa entendió lo que estamos viviendo porque ella lo vivió también. Ella fue acosada de formas grandes y pequeñas. Ella dijo,

"Cuando nos cambiamos, cambiamos el mundo."

Afortunadamente muchos de nuestros antepasados como Gloria han hecho ya mucho trabajo y mucha gente de nuestras familias y comunidades aun hacen mucho más. Están cambiando dentro de ellos mismos mientras que hagan cambios en el mundo. Están de pie en la verdad de quien son eso vale.

OPAL TOMETI
HARNAAM KAUR
Wilma Mankiller 85-95 CHIEF CHEROKEE NATION
FRED KOREMATSU
ZETTA ELLIOTT
ARSALAN IFTIKHAR
JANINE MACBETH
Bayard Rustin CIVIL RIGHTS LEADER
AUDRE LORDE
DOLORES HUERTA
LARRY ITLIONG
FANNIE LOU HAMER

I t will take time.
But together we are strong and that includes you.

Gloria Anzaldúa understood what we're going through because she went through it too. She was bullied in big and small ways. She said,

"When we change ourselves, we change the world."

Thankfully many of our ancestors like Gloria have done a lot of work already and many folks from our families and communities are doing much more. They are changing inside themselves as they are making changes out in the world. They are standing in the truth of who they are and it matters.

Estar de pie en tu verdad te mantiene fuerte.

Una de las cosas más importantes que puedes hacer como un niño es mantenerte fuerte. Párate en la verdad de quien eres. Lo más fuerte que seas lo más fuerte que es el mundo porque tú eres parte de nuestro mundo. Recuerda que tú cuentas y que lo que haces es importante.

Si ocurre bulí-ing deja a los bulís a su bulí-ing. Deja los en tu camino, aléjate y ama tu verdad – cada vez aunque solo sea un poquito. Mírate desde adentro hacia fuera. Ama la verdad que eres. Esto te mantiene fuerte. De maneras grandes y chiquitas, vale y cuenta. Hasta si es un secreto entre tú y tú. Párate en tu verdad. Párate en ti. Esto es tu base de amor.

Standing in your truth keeps you strong.

One of the most important things you can do as a kid is to keep yourself strong. Stand in the truth of who you are. The stronger you are the stronger our world is because you are a part of our world. Remember that you matter and what you do is important.

If bullying happens leave the bullies to their bullying. Walk away and love your truth-every time, even just a little. Look at yourself inside and out. Love the truth that you are. This keeps you strong. And in both the big and small ways, it matters. Even if it's just a secret between you and you, stand in your truth. Stand in you. This is your base of love.

Aquí están algunas ideas para que tu uses tu propia creatividad para parar te en tu verdad.

Tu creatividad es tuya. Es tu mayor herramienta de poder y la puedes usar para estar en tu verdad. ¡Tu creatividad te mantiene fuerte!

> Juega con dibujarte de la misma forma en que se dibujaron la gente dentro de este libro. Aquí está cada paso, a pasito y des pasito para que veas como hacerlo tú mismo. Incluye todos los detalles de ti que puedas. Hazlo que se siente como tú. Incluso, usa este dibujo de ti para que sientes cualquier y todos los sentimientos que sientes. Enojo, tristeza, miedo, felicidad, más…
>
> A través de este dibujo comparte en lo que sobresales, lo que quieres aprender, lo que ya sabes, lo que sobre vivieron tus antepasados y quien eres en tu linaje, que deseas para los niños del futuro ¡y mucho más!

Todo esto representa lo que estar de pie en tu verdad. Esto te hace quien eres. Esto y te hace fuerte.

Here are some ways that you can use your own creativity to stand in your truth.

Your creativity is yours. It is your greatest power and you can use it to stand in your truth. Your creativity keeps you strong!

> Play with drawing yourself the same way the people in this book are drawn. Here is each step slowed down so you can see how to do it yourself. Include as many details about yourself as possible. Make it feel like you. In fact you can use this drawing of yourself to feel any and all the ways you feel. Angry, sad, scared, happy, more…
>
> You can also use this drawing to share what you're good at, what you want to learn, what you already know, what your ancestors endured and who you are in your lineage, what you hope for future kids, and more!

This is what standing in your truth is. This makes you who you are. This makes you strong.

Aquí hay aún más maneras de mantenerte fuerte usando tu creatividad.

Este es un buen proyecto que hacer si has sido acosado de manera grande o chica.

Crea un dibujo que te represente pararte en tu verdad. Podrás usar la manera que aprendiste hacerlo en la última página o como sueles dibujarte.

En dibujarte, imagina algo de la naturaleza parado contigo. Una montaña. Un elefante. Un bisonte. Un cuervo. El mar. Cielo. Un árbol. Cualquier cosa que se sienta tan fuerte de la misma manera que tú te sientes o quieras sentirte fuerte. No juzgues. Puede ser lo que sea, hasta una araña o una tormenta.

Recuerda que tú eres una parte natural de todo lo que ves. Esto te mantiene fuerte y te recuerda hasta si te has olvidado por un momento quien eres. Todo incluyéndote a ti tiene propósito y pertenece en la naturaleza. Eso es la verdad.

Esto es un autorretrato con respeto a ti mismo natural.

● ◉ ●

Here are more ways to use your creativity to keep you strong.

This is a good project to do if you've been bullied in large or small ways.

Create a drawing of you standing in your truth. You can use the way you learned to draw yourself on the last page or draw how you usually draw.

When you draw yourself, imagine something from nature standing with you. A mountain. An elephant. A bison. A raven. The sea. Sky. A tree. Anything that feels strong the same way that you feel strong or want to feel strong. Don't judge. It can be anything, even a spider or a storm.

Remember that you are a natural part of everything you see. This keeps you strong and reminds you of who you are even if you have forgotten for a moment. Everything in nature has purpose and belongs including you. That is the truth.

This is a self-portrait with natural self-respect.

¿Quieres hacer más? Consigue un testigo y DEJA QUE TU RESPETO A TI MISMO SEA VISTO POR ALGUIEN RESPETOSA.

Ve decirle a tu mama, ve decirles a tus papas, o tu abuela, alguien que aprecie tu verdad y fuerza.

¿Y si por alguna razón no se lo puedas mostrar a nadie? Está bien. Sea tu propio testigo.

Si tu esta haciendo tu autorretrato debido al bulí-ing grande o penqueno, asi es como seer su propio testigo. Apuntalo tú. Si quieres se lo puedes mostrar después a alguien. Revelando lo que te ha pasado y teniendo un testigo respetuoso, aunque sea tú mismo te mantiene fuerte. Aquí tienes cuatro frases que te ayudaran a escribirlo todo.

1. Esto es lo que oí.

Escribe los nombres o palabras que oíste. Está bien escribir lo. Solo son palabras que el bulí trato de usar para que hicieras o sintieras lo que él quisiera. Te hace fuerte ver más allá de estas palabras.

2. Esto es lo que yo sé.

Escribe algo que tú sabes, por ejemplo, El bulí-ing no es verdad. Yo soy la verdad.

3. Esto es lo que yo hice.

Escribe todo lo que hayas hecho, por ejemplo: Les dije a mis papas y apunté todas las palabras. Creí un auto retrato con respeto mutuo natural y recordé que soy tan fuerte como un dragón.

4. Porque esto es quien soy.

Escribe quien eres, por ejemplo, yo soy una bella afroamericana. Yo pertenezco aquí.

Want to do more? Get a witness and LET YOUR SELF-RESPECT BE SEEN BY SOMEONE RESPECTFUL.

Go tell your mama, go tell your dads, or your nana, siblings, someone who will appreciate your truth and strength.

What if you can't show someone for some reason? That's OK.
You can be your own witness.

If you're making your self-portrait because of bullying big or small, this is how you witness yourself. You write it down. You can show it to someone later if you want. Letting out what happened and having a respectful witness keeps you strong, even if it's you. Here are 4 statements you can use to help you write everything down.

1. This is what I heard.

Write down what name or words you heard. It's OK to write them down. They are just words a bully tried to use to make you do or feel how they want. Seeing through these words keeps you strong.

2. This is what I know.

Write down something you know, for example, Bullying is not truth. I am truth.

3. This is what I did.

Write down everything you did, for example: I told my dads and wrote down all the words. I created a self portrait with natural respect and remembered I am strong like a dragon.

4. Because this is who I am.

Write down who you are, for example, I am African American and beautiful. I belong here.

i am truth
i belong
Here

Te haces más fuerte parándote en tu verdad usando autorretratos y tus palabras. Te hace fuerte tener testigo. Sentir tu circulo a tu alrededor te fortalece también.

Si es que quieres y estés listo cuando sea el tiempo propicio para ti podrás compartir con más gente que sean testigos respetuosos tus dibujos, tus palabras, tus experiencias, tu verdad. Enséñales también a tu familia y amigos de tu circulo aún más extendidos. Déjales saber que durante estos tiempos opresivos tu puedes ver más allá del bulí-ing y que conoces que tú eres la verdad. Diga les cómo estas usando tu propio poder creativo para pararte firme. Invita a otros que hagan sus propios auto retratos contigo o podrías crear retratos por tu propia cuenta de seres en tu vida. **¡La verdad crea la verdad!**

Standing in your truth through self-portraits and words makes you strong. Having a witness makes you strong. Feeling your circle around you makes you strong too.

If and when you're ready and it feels right, you can share your drawings, your words, your experiences, your truth with more people who are respectful witnesses. Show your bigger family and friends. Let them know that during these oppressive times you can see through the bullying and know that you are truth. Tell them how you're using your own creative power to stand strong. You can invite others to make self portraits with you or you can create portraits of the people in your life yourself. Truth creates truth!

Y por último, ¿y qué si no eres tú el que está siendo acosado, sino ves gente como tú siendo acosado? Esto puede ser de manera grande o chica. ¿Como apoyas la verdad y expresas respeto por tu comunidad en general cuando algo como esto ocurre?

EL ARTE HA SIDO SIEMPRE UNA MANERA EN QUE LA GENTE MUESTRA RESPETO DE UNO A OTRO. Considera la posibilidad de crear retratos de respeto por ellos. ¿Recuerdas como creaste el auto retrato con respeto natural por ti mismo? Puedes hacer lo mismo y mostrar lo que es único y fuerte sobre otra persona. Puedes hacer esto para conocidos tuyos como amigos y familiares, pero igual se los puedes hacer a gentes que ni conoces. ¡El respeto viaja con alas! De esta manera puedes usar tu poder creativo y para apoyar a ti, tus amigos, tu familia Y a tu comunidad extendida. Puedes tejer una red de la verdad más y más allá en el mundo. Tu verdad y tu poder creativo son infinitos.

And finally, what if you weren't the one being bullied, but you see people like you being bullied? This can be in big or small ways. How do you support truth and show respect for your larger community when something like this happens?

ART HAS ALWAYS BEEN A WAY FOR PEOPLE TO SHOW RESPECT FOR EACH OTHER.

Consider creating portraits of respect for them. Remember how you created the self portrait with natural respect for yourself. You can do the same thing and show what is unique and strong about another person. You can do this for folks you know like friends and family, but you can also do it for folks you've never met before. Respect travels with wings! This is a way you can use your creative power to support you, your friends and family AND your larger community. You can weave a web of truth farther and farther out into the world. Your truth and your creative power are infinite.

Always remember.

We are stronger together.

We see the truth in each other.

We focus on self love and community love first.

We use our creativity to create a new reality.

Together truth, love and creativity are rising within us.

Together we are strong.

Recuerda siempre.

Somos más fuertes juntos.

Vemos la verdad uno en sí.

Enfocamos en amor propio y amor comunitario antes de todo.

Usamos nuestra creatividad para crear una nueva realidad.

Juntos la verdad, el amor y la creatividad están creciendo
dentro de nosotros.

Juntos somos fuertes.

VOICE IS A REVOLUTION
KNOW YOUR WORDS

"BULLY" in Spanish, BULÍ: The word 'bully' from the English language is widely used in spoken language throughout Mexico and Spanglish in the US. There is no single word with the same meaning in Spanish.

People of Color or POC: is a term used primarily in the United States to describe all non-white peoples. It originated with the Black Women's Agenda in Houston, Texas in 1977 at the National Women's Conference. The BWA, still in existence today, created a term that included other non-African American women to call out the widespread experience of racism.

Chicano/a/x: is a term of pride popularized in the 60's civil rights era for people of Mexican descent born in America to acknowledge their indigenous roots.

Native American/American Indian: Both terms are used for various reasons and are appropriate, however most preferable would be to use a person's tribal nation. Please note that American Indians are not 'people of color' or 'ethnic' populations. They are indigenous people with dual citizenship to their own nation and the US.

Indigenous: means originating from a particular place. Indigenous peoples are also called first people, aboriginal people and native people.

LGBTQI2S: Lesbian Gay Bisexual Transgender Queer Intersex 2Spirit

Colonization: in the USA and much of the Americas is based on Europeans stealing land and resources by killing, enslaving, corralling, dominating and using Indigenous and African people to increase their prosperity. This history effects present day life in multiple ways, including what and how history is taught.

Slavery: is complete ownership and control of a human being by another human being using force and power. Slavery became legal in the US in 1641 for Africans and indigenous Americans and did not legally end until 1865. The repercussions and persistent social impact have never been fully addressed and resolved and much of our history has been suppressed.

Racism: is discrimination or prejudice against someone based on their race or ethnicity. This is the false belief that all members of a racial or ethnic group possess characteristics or abilities specific to that group, especially to judge the group as 'better or less than' another. The truth is there is no difference between human beings. While possessing different skills and experiences, all humans are equal.

Ableism: is discrimination and prejudice against people with disabilities. This ranges from social interaction to education access to public and private architecture and design and more.

Sexism: is discrimination and prejudice against someone based on their identity as a girl or woman. This is the false belief that boy or male identities are superior and promotes negative stereotypes and restrictive gender roles for all people, including transgender people and people who do not fit into the gender binary of only male and female.

Anti-Semitism: is discrimination and prejudice against Jews. There is a long history in Europe of severe oppression of Jewish people including the loss of an estimated 6 million Jews during WWII. Although this book focuses on People of Color and Indigenous People in America, it is important to include that Jews are also oppressed in America.

Homophobia: is the discrimination and prejudice against gay, lesbian, bisexual and 2Spirit people. This is the false belief that heterosexuality is normal and homosexuality is not. The truth is that homosexuality has existed for as long as heterosexuality has and both are a perfectly normal part of nature.

Transphobia: is the discrimination and prejudice against transgender people or people who do not fit into the gender binary of only male and female. Transgender people and gender fluid people, like homosexuals have always existed and are a perfectly normal part of nature.

Islamaphobia: is the discrimination and prejudice against Islam or Muslims. Islam is the second most popular religion in the world and is based on the teachings of Mohammad in the Quran. Sometimes Sikhs are mistaken for Muslims, however Sikhs are generally of Indian descent, not Middle Eastern and are part of an entirely different tradition.

Misogyny: is the basic dislike and judgment against people who identify as women and girls.

Oppression: is one group of people using power in an unfair and inhumane way in a society in order to bully another group of people to keep them unbalanced and without resources thereby more able to be controlled.

Privilege: is a socially embedded form of bullying that gives special rights or advantages to a particular group of people and not others that usually rises from how a country or culture develops. For the non-privileged this impacts confidence, relaxation, a sense of belonging and value. Everyone can become aware of what privilege we have in the world and personally work toward greater balance and equity between people.

Equity: is about people getting what they need to be equally successful with all other people. Because people are beginning from different positions what some people need is different from what other people need. Whereas equality is about everyone being treated the same as each other. Right now people are not beginning from the same position so being treated equally is not yet fair.

STRONGER TOGETHER
KNOW YOUR MOVEMENTS:

Black Lives Matter: www.blacklivesmatter.com

Standing Rock: www.standwithstandingrock.net

Women's Movement:
www.nwhp.org/resources/womens-rights-movement/history-of-the-womens-rights-movement
www.womensmarch.com

Immigrants' Rights: www.aclu.org/issues/immigrants-rights | www.islamophobia.org

 Disability Rights: www.adapt.org

   LGBTQ Rights & Pride: www.gaypridecalendar.com | www.transequality.org
www.lambdalegal.org

   Resistance 101 (Teach-Ins): www.teachingforchange.org/resistance101

NEVER ALONE
KNOW YOUR PEOPLE:
(pgs. 15, 28-29, a small sampling of ancestors and community activists and artists)

Alicia Garza – African American activist of Mexican American and African American descent widely acclaimed for her activism, cofounder Black Lives Matter.

Opal Tometi – Nigerian American writer, strategist and community organizer, widely acclaimed activist for immigrants' rights, cofounder Black Lives Matter.

Patrisse Cullors – African American artist, organizer and widely acclaimed freedom fighter, named NAACP History Maker, cofounder Black Lives Matter.

Isa Noyola – Translatina activist, national leader in LGBT immigrant rights movement and director of programs at Transgender Law Center.

James Baldwin – African American, gay novelist, essayist, playwright, poet and social critic. 2017 Oscar-nominated documentary *I Am Not Your Negro* highlights Baldwin's work and perspective on racism in America.

Barbara Cameron and Randy Burns – cofounded Gay American Indians, the first Native gay and lesbian group to educate the world on Indigenous LGBTQ people and contributing to the Two Spirit Movement.

Gloria Anzaldúa – Queer Chicana poet, writer and cultural, feminist and queer theorist, activist and children's book author. Widely acclaimed for her work.

Bayard Rustin – African American, gay civil rights strategist and organizer, organized the March on Washington from behind the scenes and helped mold Martin Luther King Jr. into an international symbol of peace. He brought Gandhi's practice of peaceful resistance to the American Civil Rights Movement.

Audre Lorde – Black writer, feminist, womanist, lesbian, civil rights activist. *"For the master's tools will never dismantle the master's house. They may allow us temporarily to beat him at his own game, but they will never enable us to bring about genuine change."*

Louise Erdrich – Turtle Mountain Band of Chippewa Indians, widely acclaimed award-winning American author, including children's books featuring Native American characters and settings.

Winona LaDuke – Ojibwe Nation, American environmentalist, economist, writer, first Native American woman to receive an electoral vote for Vice President.

Wilma Mankiller – First female chief of the Cherokee Nation, lifelong activist for Native American and women's rights.

Cesar Chavez – Mexican American labor leader and civil rights activist founded National Farm Workers Association.

Dolores Huerta – Mexican American activist cofounded the National Farm Workers Association (NFWA) later the United Farm Workers. She has won numerous awards for her work.

Pat Mora – Mexican American, Latina award-winning author of poetry, nonfiction and children's books. Founded *Dia de Los Niños, Day of the Children*, a community-based, family literacy initiative based on the Mexican National Children's Day festivities tradition now celebrated throughout the US.

Malala Yousafzai – Pakistani advocate for girls' education was shot in the head by extremists in 2012. She survived without serious brain damage and became the youngest person to win the Nobel Peace Prize. Read her autobiography, *I Am Malala: The Girl Who Stood Up for Education and Was Shot by the Taliban.*

Harnaam Kaur – British Sikh woman breaking societal norms and challenging conventional beauty norms, body positivity activist, Guinness world record for youngest woman with a beard.

Arsalan Iftikhar – Muslim American international human rights lawyer, global media commentator and author promoting global awareness and peace.

Fred Korematsu – Japanese American civil rights hero refused to be incarcerated in the Japanese Internment camps and took his case to the Supreme Court. With new evidence previously hidden, he won his case in 1983. Received the Presidential Medal of Freedom.

Grace Lee Boggs – Chinese American author, social activist, philosopher and feminist, founded Detroit Summer an organization working to transform communities through youth leadership, creativity and collective action.

Larry Itliong – Filipino American labor organizer and considered 'one of the fathers of the West Coast labor movement.' He led the first strikes known as the Delano Grape Strike.

Janine Macbeth – Multiracial artist, author, publisher and social justice activist. Founded Blood Orange Press, committed to books that recognize and affirm first nations and kids of color, and their power and potential in the world.

Zetta Elliott – Black feminist writer of poetry, plays, essays, novels and award-winning children's book author. Founded Rosetta Press, committed to publishing books that reveal, explore, and foster a Black feminist vision of the world.

Fannie Lou Hamer – African American voting rights activist, civil rights leader and philanthropist. Cofounded the Mississippi Freedom Democratic Party.

Rosa Parks – African American civil rights activist, refused to surrender her bus seat to a white passenger spurring the Montgomery boycott and other efforts to end segregation.

Claudette Colvin – African American 15 year old girl who refused to give up her seat to a white passenger on a public bus setting the stage for Rosa Parks.

TRUTH IN HISTORY
KNOW YOUR BASICS:

US history:
www.zinnedproject.org/materials/indigenous-peoples-history-of-the-us

American Indians in Children's Literature:
www.americanindiansinchildrensliterature.blogspot.com

Economy dependent on slavery:
www.historyisaweapon.com/defcon1/zinnslaem10.html

President Slave Statistics (pg. 11):
www.wikipedia.org/wiki/List_of_Presidents_of_the_United_States_who_owned_slaves

More resources on our website:
www.reflectionpress.com/truth

CPSIA information can be obtained at www.ICGtesting.com
Printed in the USA
BVIW12n1921100317
478066BV00005B/103